P9-CFO-501

HOLOCAUST BIOGRAPHIES

Emmanuel Ringelblum

Historian of the Warsaw Ghetto

Mark Beyer

THE ROSEN PUBLISHING GROUP, INC.
NEW YORK

Published in 2001 by The Rosen Publishing Group, Inc.
29 East 21st Street, New York, NY 10010

First Edition

Library of Congress Cataloging-in-Publication Data

Beyer, Mark.
Emmanuel Ringelblum: historian of the Warsaw ghetto / By Mark Beyer.
p. cm. — (Holocaust biographies)
Includes bibliographical references (p.) and index.
ISBN 0-8239-3375-X
1. Ringelblum, Emanuel, 1900–1944. 2. Jews—Poland—Warsaw—Biography 3. Holocaust, Jewish (1939–1945)—Poland—Warsaw—Biography. 4. Jewish historians—Poland—Warsaw—Biography 5. Warsaw (Poland)—Biography.
[1. Ringelblum, Emanuel, 1900–1944. 2. Jews—Poland—Warsaw. 3. Holocaust, Jewish (1939–1945)—Poland—Warsaw.]
I. Title. II. Series.
DS135.P63 R563 2001
940.53'18'092—dc21

2001002040

Manufactured in the United States of America

Contents

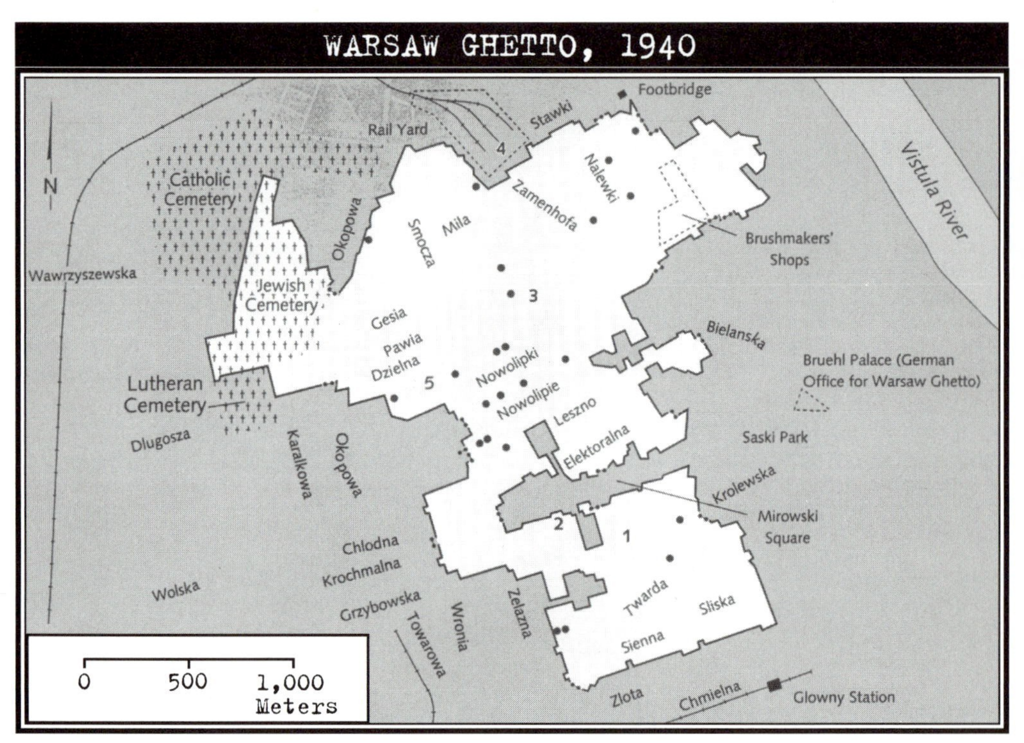

— Ghetto boundary, November 15, 1940: wall with barbed wire on top

Entrances, gates to ghetto

● Selected ghetto factories

1. Jewish Council *(Judenrat)*
2. Jewish police
3. Pawiak prison
4. *Umschlagplatz*
5. Hiding place of Oneg Shabbat archive

Introduction

Three metal boxes lay beneath the rubble of the Warsaw ghetto after World War II (1939–1945) ended. Buried since 1942, the boxes held papers, photographs, documents, and journals. This archive told the short but brutal history of Nazi crimes against Polish Jews, specifically the Jews of the Warsaw ghetto.

Thirty-three-year-old Emmanuel Ringelblum started this archive in 1933. Ringelblum was a Jewish historian born and raised in Poland. When news came of Adolf Hitler's rise to power in Germany, Ringelblum knew that Europe and European Jews would experience great terror. He began collecting all sorts of materials that would record Nazi crimes. He also kept a journal to describe what he saw. Later, others would help Ringelblum collect eyewitness accounts of Nazi crimes against Jews.

The Nazis executed Ringelblum in 1944. He and the group of people who had helped create the archive seemed to know what would become of them. They were known as Oneg Shabbat ("Sabbath Celebrants"). The Oneg Shabbat members buried the archive in several metal tins and milk jugs just months before the Nazis destroyed the Warsaw ghetto.

Many Polish Jews knew that these boxes had been buried. After the war, ghetto survivors wanted to find these metal boxes to show the world what the Nazis had done to the Jews of Poland.

Almost nothing was left of Warsaw after the war ended. The Nazis had destroyed large parts of the city when they defeated Poland in September 1939. Although the Nazis retreated to Germany in 1945, they had fought fiercely for every inch of land. As the Soviet army pushed the Nazis to Berlin, it destroyed almost all that was left of Warsaw.

Holocaust survivors pose atop the rubble of a bunker in the former Warsaw ghetto in July 1945.

There was one part of Warsaw the Russians could not destroy, however. The Nazis had already bombed it and burned it. This section of Warsaw was the Jewish ghetto, where the Nazis confined nearly 400,000 European Jews (mostly Polish) beginning in 1940. Two years later, less than 60,000 still lived. The others had been carried away in railway boxcars to the Treblinka death camp only sixty miles away.

There, most of the ghetto Jews were stripped of their clothing and possessions and were gassed to death in special rooms. Afterward, their bodies were burned in ovens. The Nazis wanted to kill all European Jews and remove all traces of the crime.

Treblinka and the other death camps were discovered by U.S., British, and Soviet armies. At first, these soldiers could not understand what had really taken place in the camps. They could not understand why the Nazis would kill civilians with such brutality. How had this happened? How could the world allow this to happen? Some of the answers lay in the three metal boxes buried beneath the remains of the city of Warsaw.

A year after the war ended, Warsaw still lay in ruins. Polish Jews worked to help rebuild their crushed capital. While digging up the area that was once the ghetto, some workers struck metal with their shovels. They uncovered one metal box. It held volumes of written notes, newspapers, documents, and photographs. The

The efforts of Emmanuel Ringelblum and his Oneg Shabbat companions were hidden in milk cans and tin boxes shortly before the Warsaw ghetto was destroyed.

workers knew these papers must be important. Part of the Oneg Shabbat archive had been discovered. The second box, containing more archive material, was found four years later, in 1950. The third part has yet to be found.

Inside the first box were Ringelblum's notes from the Warsaw ghetto. The notes were perhaps the most important part of the archive. Ringelblum had a gift for capturing the important moments of Nazi occupation.

A scene:
An auto with Others [the word Ringelblum used to identify Nazis] riding in it comes along. A Jewish hand wagon blocks the way at Karmelicka Street. The car can't move. One of the Others gets out and begins beating the Jew. A shudder runs down the Jew's back. A man in the car calls out: "Let him alone. He's contagious." The attacker reconsiders and lets the Jew be.

Taken from the Oneg Shabbat archive

Ringelblum's *Notes from the Warsaw Ghetto* was published in 1958. The book's publication proved that the Nazis had failed to hide their murders.

Early on, Ringelblum saw Nazism as a powerful force against all humanity, but especially against Jews. He wanted the world to learn what had happened to Poland's Jews. Yet when he wrote his first journal entry six years before the Nazis invaded Poland, Ringelblum had no idea just how deadly the Nazis would become to Jews and to the people of Europe and the rest of the world.

1. Hitler, World War II, and the Holocaust

In 1932, the National Socialist German Workers' Party, or Nazis, held many seats in the Reichstag (German congress). That gave them power in ruling Germany. In 1933, Nazi leader Adolf Hitler was named chancellor by the government. He quickly seized control of Germany.

To win support, the Nazis had promised jobs to German voters. They declared that Germany would again become a European power. Many Germans liked what they heard from the Nazis. They remembered their defeat in World War I (1914–1918) and how they were forced to pay war costs to the victorious French, British, and Americans as part of the Treaty of Versailles. Many Germans were out of work during the 1920s, and a worldwide economic depression in 1929 further hurt the German economy. Germans were humiliated and angry. By 1932, they were looking for someone to lead them back to power. They found that person in Adolf Hitler.

In order to hold on to power, Hitler needed to get rid of his enemies. He ordered the Nazi Party to pass laws that lessened the Reichstag's power. Hitler declared "emergency" power and placed the country under military rule. The Nazi Party gave him the name "Führer," or leader.

Hitler outlawed all political parties except the Nazi Party. The Nazis took over newspapers, magazines, radio stations, and movie companies. German citizens were given only the information that Hitler and the Nazis wanted them to hear and know. This type of information, called propaganda, was used to spread lies about communists, foreign countries, and German Jews. Magazines printed fake stories of Jewish treachery. Radio stations broadcast false stories about communist plots against the German government. Thousands of people were arrested and placed in concentration camps. Thousands more were murdered.

Hitler wanted German citizens to believe the lies his government told them. He wanted Germans to fear Jews, communists, and foreigners so that they would hate these groups. Once Germans began to hate, they

Nazis and civilians salute Hitler during his rise to power in Germany.

would want to fight. Hitler wanted Germans to fight for him—more specifically, for his plans to expand German territory. Hitler wanted Germany to have *Lebensraum*, or living space.

To expand Germany, Hitler had to go to war with neighboring countries. The lies poured from German radios and newspapers while Hitler planned for war. After only a few months, Germans began to believe the lies they heard. And then they began to hate. A few years later, when World War II was about to begin, many Germans wanted to take revenge on Germany's enemies because they had believed all the lies fed to them over the years. Those who saw through the Nazi lies could not do anything to stop the coming war.

One of the biggest lies that Hitler spread was that Jews were the source of all Germany's problems. He had written out his case against Jews in a book he published in 1925. In *Mein Kampf*—translated as "my struggle"—Hitler blamed Jewish industrialists for losing World War I. He thought Jewish-owned businesses should be owned by Germans. He blamed Jewish bankers for causing the Great Depression. He blamed Jews for trying to destroy the "pure" blood of Germans by marrying non-Jewish Germans. Pure Germans, or "Aryans," were the people Hitler said he was trying to protect. The Nazis wanted no Jew to have any influence over Germany. Hitler spread his lies and hatred for Jews for seven years before he took office. Once in power, Hitler continued to direct his hate toward the Jews; the German people continued to hail him as their leader.

The Nazis passed laws that took Jewish businesses and gave them to the government. The government handed the businesses over to non-Jewish Germans. Jews working in the German government were fired. Jewish teachers were pulled from colleges and schools across the country. Soon, Jewish students could not even attend college, and Jewish children could not go to school. By 1935, 75,000 German Jews had fled the

Members of the German *Sturmabteilung* (SA), Hitler's street agitators, ride through Berlin in April of 1933 calling for boycotts of Jewish businesses.

country. That left more than 400,000 Jews at the mercy of Hitler and the Nazis.

Those who fled to other countries were sometimes not welcomed. German propaganda and anti-Semitism (anti-Jewish feeling) had already spread to Austria and to Poland, which was home to the largest number of Jews in Europe. In 1936, Polish laws began to strip Jews of the same rights that they had lost in Germany. Tens of thousands of Polish Jews fled their homeland.

In Germany, the Nazis imprisoned thousands of Jews in concentration camps. German communists, college professors, religious leaders, and mentally impaired people were also thrown into these camps. Prisoners were beaten, forced to work without food, and murdered. The Nazis were killing their own people—Germans—simply because they were Jewish or part of these other groups.

There was nothing the Jews could do to fight Nazi laws. Although some individuals and small groups tried, Nazi police forces—the SS and Gestapo—quickly imprisoned or killed protesters. Few Germans spoke against Nazi brutality. Too many had already accepted the ever-present propaganda against the Jews. The lives of Germans had improved under Nazi rule; many were willing to ignore the Jews' suffering in return for this improvement in their own lives.

In 1939, Germany invaded Poland, starting World War II. Great Britain and France declared war in return, but Hitler didn't care. In Poland he could continue his program of Jewish persecution with few outsiders watching. The Nazis began building dozens of concentration camps in Poland.

Hundreds of thousands of Jews were rounded up in Germany, Austria, Czechoslovakia, and Poland. In an effort to isolate Jews, the Nazis forced them into concentration camps or ghettos (separate areas within towns). Life was brutal; food was in short supply. Hitler intended to work the Jews to death.

Jews were used for slave labor, working in factories or building roads. Some were put to work digging holes just to fill them up again. Thousands of women and children were murdered because they could not be used for work. Thousands more were too old to work. They were lined up next to deep holes and shot. Their bodies were buried in mass graves.

It was only later, in 1942, that Hitler and his officers began the "Final Solution"—their plan to kill all the Jews in Europe by gassing them and burning their bodies in crematoriums. Special camps were built for this purpose alone. They were called death camps. Under the secrecy of war, the Nazis killed six million Jews by working, starving, gassing, or shooting them to death.

At the war's end, when the Allied armies had defeated the Germans, soldiers from the United States, France, Britain, the Soviet Union, and other countries rescued Jews from the

U.S. Congressman Ed V. Izak, a member of a house delegation to Germany to view evidence of Nazi crimes, looks at human remains in a crematorium in 1945.

concentration camps. What they saw was horrific. The surviving Jews looked like skeletons because they had been starved. Open pits held thousands of rotting bodies. Some ovens used to burn gassed Jews still held the bones of the victims. Concentration camp survivors called these years of murder the Holocaust.

Jewish Ghettos

Before the Final Solution began, the Nazis wanted to keep their eyes on Jews living in Germany and in the countries Germany had conquered. They hated the Jews and wanted them separated from German life. Work camps housed many thousands of Jews and other "criminals" used for forced labor. Yet there were so many Jews that camps could not be built to hold all of them. Therefore, the Nazis separated parts of towns and cities to house Jews. They built walls and fences around blocks of buildings. These ghettos became Jewish prisons.

Jews were kept in ghettos and not allowed to mix with the rest of the city's citizens. Jewish ghettos existed in Germany, Austria, Czechoslovakia, Estonia, Latvia, Lithuania, and Poland. Jews living in cities where ghettos existed were forced from their homes and sent into the ghettos. Jews living in small towns or on farms were taken into the city ghettos. Ghetto residents were unable to earn a living or go to school outside the ghetto, and they could not leave its confines, except to work in forced labor groups.

The most infamous Jewish ghetto was in Warsaw, the capital of Poland. The city held more than 300,000 Jews—the largest number of Jews living in any city in Europe. After the Nazis defeated Poland in September of 1939, Hitler ordered that all Warsaw Jews were to be kept in one part of the city. Warsaw was actually divided into three sections: one for Germans, one for Poles, and one for Jews. The north section of the city became the Warsaw ghetto. Brick walls separated one hundred

Nazi officials inspect the wall surrounding the Warsaw ghetto.

square city blocks from the rest of the city. After being robbed of their homes and possessions, the Jews had little left to carry into the ghetto. Rich and poor alike were taken and pushed into apartment buildings to live or die together.

The Jews' reaction to imprisonment surprises people today. Almost immediately, the Jews living in the Warsaw ghetto began cultural programs to keep themselves busy and to continue living as best they could; tens of thousands were not working at all. Emmanuel Ringelblum was responsible for organizing many groups and committees. Plays were staged in storefronts, music concerts were performed in vacant halls, and dances were organized for young and old. Education programs were quickly begun as well. Children were sent to schools in apartments or unused offices. Teachers who were no longer allowed to teach outside the ghetto taught classes. Small newspapers began to appear on the streets reporting news from the outside.

These events of ordinary life occurred without much interference from the Nazis. This gave Warsaw Jews a false sense of hope. Violence was all around them. People were shot for arguing with soldiers. Smugglers were shot if caught bringing in goods from the outside. Homeless men, women, and children were found frozen to death on the streets after cold winter nights. The Warsaw ghetto was a place where people lived, but it was a place overwhelmed by death. Every day, thousands of Jews left the ghetto for forced labor in factories or outside the city; each day hundreds did not return.

At that time, little information from Germany or other occupied countries reached the outside world. There were rumors about additional anti-Jewish laws, beatings, and murders. Since the Nazis held power over all media, the only sources of real news were reports from people who had escaped.

Inside the Nazi world, however, many Jews were keeping written records of Nazi crimes. Emmanuel Ringelblum had been keeping records for seven years already. By January 1940, Ringelblum was living in the ghetto, where he began recruiting others to help him keep records and gather documents. Ringelblum saw this work as his job—maybe his last. His mission was to make sure that one day the outside world would learn the truth of Nazi brutality and murder.

2. Student and Activist

It is only fitting that Emmanuel Ringelblum was the designer of the archive that taught the world about Jewish life under Nazi rule. His hard work as a teacher and social activist was widely known years before World War II began. He was also recognized as an important Jewish scholar and historian.

Ringelblum had several opportunities to escape war-torn Poland and the Warsaw ghetto. But when many Jewish leaders and colleagues fled Nazi persecution for safety in other countries, he made the choice to stay. Ringelblum understood the instinct to flee, but he also knew that millions of Jews could not leave. It was for those people, trapped by the brutality of Nazism, that Ringelblum stayed in Warsaw. His education was based in Jewish history, and he was all too aware of the horrors that European Jews had experienced through the ages. In 1939, Ringelblum knew that another great storm had descended upon Europe. As a writer, activist, historian, and man of his generation, Ringelblum felt a tremendous responsibility to help his people in any way that he could.

Always a Student

Emmanuel Ringelblum was born in 1900 in an area of Poland that was part of the Austro-Hungarian Empire. Poland had not been an independent country since 1830 and would not see independence again until 1918. Nonetheless, Ringelblum learned the Polish language in school and came from a Polish-Jewish heritage. His family had once been wealthy, but by 1918 was poor and living in the small town of Nowy Sancsz.

Ringelblum worked his way through school while living with his parents. He was very busy each day, but he was a strong student and a hard worker. He would attend classes from early morning until two in the afternoon. Afterward, Ringelblum tutored other students until evening. Only then could he attend to his own schoolwork. Even this hectic schedule was not enough to tire the maturing scholar. Ringelblum also found time to be a member of a self-education group sponsored by the Labor Zionist movement to which he belonged. It seemed that Ringelblum was always trying to learn more.

Such strong educational goals drove Ringelblum to organize evening classes for day workers. His social-consciousness was already proving to be of great benefit to the community.

Ringelblum enrolled in the University of Warsaw in 1919 and left for the city that fall. This was just after the end of World War I, and Poland had again become an independent nation. Ringelblum enjoyed the sense of nationalism that came with the reunification of his country, but he also observed that Jews were discriminated against by Poles and the Polish government. Poland was made up of lands once part of Russia, Hungary, and Germany, and each of these former empires had a history of anti-Semitism. Their discrimination, hatred, and murderous acts toward Jews carried over into the newly formed Poland.

In order to pay for his own schooling, Ringelblum taught courses through the Central Jewish School Organization of Poland (CJSO). Having little money, Ringelblum often experienced hunger firsthand. But he was driven to prove himself a worthy teacher in the community, and his hard work and dedication were recognized when he was appointed principal of an evening school in Warsaw. Later, he became the chairman of the educational council that oversaw all five evening schools.

The hundreds of students that Ringelblum taught admired him. As education council chair, Ringelblum formed a student club that met on Saturday afternoons and on evenings when there were no classes. Ringelblum also gave lectures and taught special-interest classes. All of this work was in addition to his studies at the University of Warsaw.

Ringelblum began his college career studying economics, but he soon turned to sociology. Eventually, he found that he liked history best. Because of his background, he worked toward

Jewish students attend class in a Polish gymnasium in 1938.

becoming a social, rather than a political, historian. The difference between the two is the focus put on historical events: Political history focuses on politics, leaders, and power, while social history focuses on people living and working under political systems. Given his social activism, it is no wonder that Ringelblum found his passion in studying people. This training would prove vital to Ringelblum's work on the Oneg Shabbat archives.

Ringelblum's energy and social drive did not stop with his teaching. At the university, he was the leader of the General Academic Federation of Jewish Students. This growing group of young intellectuals argued for and received reduced tuition fees from the government. The federation was a large group that helped the community, and Ringelblum became active in its programs. He assisted the federation's self-aid program. This program ran a soup kitchen for the homeless and the poor, managed a free loan society, and developed other social programs.

In order to accommodate all of his activities, Ringelblum had to extend the time spent on his education. He did not earn his doctorate until 1927. His dissertation was titled "History of the Jews in Warsaw up to the Expulsion of 1527." Ringelblum knew of the hardships that Jews had faced during their 3000-year history—long before the Nazis came to power. In 1932, the Warsaw section of the Polish Historical Society published his dissertation. His work immediately won praise from historians and colleagues.

This was a time of great success for Ringelblum, but it was also a time for concern. After World War I, and with the reformation of Poland, the seeds of Polish anti-Semitism were growing. Regulations and laws against Jews were a part of government and private practice. Few felt this more directly than Ringelblum himself. Although he was recognized within the community as a gifted teacher, he was unable to teach at the university simply because he was a Jew. Because this was the way all Jews were being treated, Ringelblum had no other choice but to accept this slap in his face.

Ringelblum did not let such a crisis interrupt his goals. In fact, he hardly viewed it as a crisis. He was a teacher and historian, and there was always work for someone like him. He couldn't have imagined, however, the work that he would eventually be driven to do.

Changing Times: 1927–1939

After earning his doctorate, Ringelblum stayed on in Warsaw and taught history in a secondary school. While teaching, he continued his research and writing. During the next twelve years, he would write dozens of articles and three more books on European history, Jewish history, and Polish-Jewish relations.

All of his writing was based on researching original sources. This made his work important to scholars but challenging for himself as a historian. To learn the histories of people and events, Ringelblum had to dig through many court records and council meeting notes. This was hard work, but it was work that helped all historians. Ringelblum was able to bring to life the people and events of nearly forgotten times. His focus, as always, was human beings and what they meant to society.

A major part of Ringelblum's life and work was devoted to Jewish activism within Poland. Since Jews were largely restricted from taking part in Polish life and politics, Ringelblum helped them create their own society. He found time to develop sports clubs, choirs, dramatic groups, music circles, libraries, and summer camps, and he assisted in the administration of night classes for adults in 165 towns throughout Poland.

Ringelblum's role as teacher and social activist made it natural for him to take part in politics. He did this through his membership in the left-wing Labor Zionist movement.

Ringelblum prided himself on never missing one of his party's public gatherings.

Ringelblum's work was for the good of the people and Polish society. Yet in 1933, Ringelblum saw change happening. Adolf Hitler had risen to power in Germany. As chancellor, Hitler began a system of terrorism against his enemies and German Jews. Hitler's irrational discrimination against Jews was based on hate-mongering that had its roots in history and that was heightened by Nazi propaganda.

In June of 1933, Ringelblum began a personal journal. In it, he recorded Nazi crimes against Jews taking place in Germany. He expressed his thoughts and wrote down what he saw. He began to collect photographs, letters, documents, and posters. He also noted actions that Jews took to challenge laws that discriminated against them.

During the summer of 1933, Polish Jews took a stand by boycotting German-made products. Jewish students protested Germany's anti-Jewish laws by throwing stink bombs in theaters showing German films.

The June 26 edition of the Nazi Party newspaper boldly called for all Jews to be expelled from Germany. But the newspaper didn't stop there. The Nazis declared that Jews "can never be anything but stateless aliens, and they can never have any legal or

Germans boycotted Jewish businesses. The slogan here reads "Whoever buys from Jews is a traitor to the people."

constitutional status." These words were a signal to Ringelblum that Jews had many things to fear in the future. He hoped European Jews could hold out until Hitler's power crumbled. Until then, Ringelblum continued to gather material.

Terror Builds

Anti-Jewish crimes began to increase throughout eastern Europe. Many Polish townspeople and peasants believed all the hate talk about Jews. Jewish townspeople and farmers began to fear for their lives.

In 1936, the Polish government passed a law requiring all business owners to put their names on their signs. This made the ownership of the business easy to identify. Crimes against Jewish businesses and business owners began to happen frequently. Windows were smashed, goods were stolen, and Jewish business owners were beaten in the streets.

Thousands of Jews left Poland, fearing for their safety. Ringelblum stayed and tried to help stop the growing anti-Jewish feelings of his fellow citizens. His social activism grew. Ringelblum joined the American Joint Distribution Committee, a Jewish self-help organization. He also worked to set up a Warsaw section of the Yiddish Scientific Institute. Soon after, he became the chairman of the Young Historians Circle.

During the last week of August 1939, while Ringelblum was in Geneva, Switzerland, for the twenty-first World Jewish Congress, which met each year to discuss Jewish issues, news broke that the German army had gathered along the Polish border. Many delegates did not return to Poland, deciding instead to flee to Palestine, France, or Great Britain.

Ringelblum and other delegates from his party chose to return to Warsaw, traveling by train through Italy and Yugoslavia. Their journey back home was dangerous. In Hungary, they received a police escort to the

Polish border, and then they traveled to Warsaw on a train. By now the Germans had invaded Poland. German planes bombed the train carrying Ringelblum's group, but they arrived safely, and the next day Ringelblum was back at work. He would not let the Nazis command his life.

3. Warsaw and the Ghetto

Emmanuel Ringelblum was thirty-nine years old when the Nazis invaded Poland, in September 1939. His wife, Yehudit, who came from a middle-class Warsaw family, worked as a schoolteacher in the neighborhood. With their seven-year-old son, Uri, they lived in a large apartment on Leszno Street in the Jewish Quarter. There, they often entertained friends, and sometimes they offered their extra room to out-of-town visitors.

Ringelblum was five feet ten inches tall with black hair and a memorable smile. He was by all accounts a happy man who loved to laugh and tell jokes. He also enjoyed telling friends the funny things that young Uri had

Ringelblum with his son, Uri, in Poland, in 1938

said to him that morning or the day before. This happiness behind the hardworking lifestyle is apparent in photographs of the historian, in which he seems relaxed and confident. A patient man, he believed in the importance of his work. Soon, Ringelblum would need to draw upon both traits.

Poland Falls

Six days after the invasion, German forces surrounded Warsaw. Tens of thousands of Poles and Jews fled the city. Jews were especially frightened for their lives; they had heard and read about Nazi murders within Germany. They did not doubt that Hitler's killers would do the same to Polish Jews.

Emmanuel Ringelblum had the chance to escape Warsaw and Poland. He chose to stay with his people. He knew the social agencies he worked for would be desperately needed once the Germans took control of Poland. Warsaw had been bombed; people were homeless and hungry. Ringelblum's social agencies could help people pick up the pieces of their damaged lives.

Ringelblum also wanted to continue documenting Nazi crimes against Jews. He felt that Warsaw was the place where he was needed. He could not be a historian of his people from the safety of a foreign country. He and his family would stay.

Within six weeks, the Germans won the battle for Poland. The Nazis quickly subjected Polish Jews to the same laws that German Jews had lived under for six years. Polish Jews lost their jobs in government and teaching. Jewish doctors and lawyers were refused work. Many Jewish businesses were taken over by the government and given to non-Jewish Poles or Germans.

Polish Jews had to make a list of all their possessions. They had to declare how much money they kept in banks. The Nazis collected these lists and began to steal from the Jews whenever they liked. Nazis would often go into a building and break down the door of a Jewish family's apartment. They would steal gold or cash from the family. Sometimes they murdered one of the family members.

Nazi SS troops beat Jews in the streets. Polish anti-Semites were allowed to harass, rob, and terrorize Jews with no fear of the consequences. Jewish-owned stores had their windows smashed and goods robbed. Rabbis were humiliated by being made to wash

This Jewish-owned shop was destroyed during the anti-Jewish riots in Stanislawow, Poland, in April 1935.

sidewalks using their prayer shawls. Hasidic Jews were tormented and humiliated when Nazi soldiers and Polish citizens cut off their ear locks. Jewish mothers and children were forced to clean streets while Poles, Germans, and Nazi soldiers watched and laughed.

September 24–29: The Game
In a certain building where Jews are working, They [Ringelblum's reference to Nazis] look through the telephone book for addresses of Jewish professionals. Finding a professional, they enter his apartment, keep him there all day, and leave at night. All this to terrorize them. They beat up people for saluting Them ("I'm no friend of yours"). And they beat up people for not saluting them. Sometimes both things happen to the same person.

Taken from the Oneg Shabbat archive

Thousands of Jews were forced into labor groups or taken to labor camps. The

Nazis rationed all food, and Jews were given starvation rations. For identification purposes, all Jews were forced to wear the Star of David (a Jewish symbol) on their clothing. The defeated Polish government did little to help. The Jews of Poland were alone.

Ringelblum recorded all sorts of these events in his journal. This was a new kind of notebook, however. In it, Ringelblum continued to write down all that he saw, but now he included eyewitness accounts from people who came to Warsaw from around Poland and beyond.

When the Nazis began deporting German Jews to Poland, Ringelblum's role in the Jewish Defense Council (JDC) increased. At the same time, Polish Jews from across the nation were taken from their homes and brought to Warsaw and other cities to live in ghettos. The JDC helped the refugees with money, food, and clothes. Since Ringelblum spoke German, he was able to speak with the refugees as they poured into the city. He quietly interviewed these terrorized people.

I had daily lively contact with everything that was happening. News came to me of every event affecting Jews in Warsaw and its suburbs. Almost every day I saw delegations from the Polish provinces.

Taken from the Oneg Shabbat archive

Ringelblum noted that many died during the long journey to Warsaw. Many people had walked hundreds of miles. Starvation was common. Murders from beatings and shootings were frequent. When Ringelblum went to the German occupation offices to plead that the relief work continue, he was beaten until he bled. He returned to his office and continued working.

Of course, if he were caught with a notebook, the Nazis would kill him. Any record keeping or note taking was illegal. If Nazis found evidence of books or writing, the sentence was death. Ringelblum knew this, but still he recorded all he saw and whatever he could get people to tell him.

Forming Oneg Shabbat

The eyewitness accounts that Ringelblum recorded each night were the beginning of the ghetto archive. Ringelblum quickly realized, however, that he needed help with his work. It was not enough to record all that he saw and all that he could learn from refugees himself; he needed others to help write, interview, collect documents, and organize everything. Photographs, handbills, posters—even the daily decrees that were nailed to telephone poles—all must be collected and organized.

Ringelblum knew that others were keeping journals of events, too. Refugees coming from other cities had notebooks hidden in their clothes. Doctors, teachers, and even children had taken time to write about their daily miseries under Nazi occupation. Almost immediately, he began recruiting people to help him.

Since he was a social historian, Ringelblum was very well suited to organize a group to keep an archive. A proven writer who knew how to evaluate documents and choose the most important ones to keep, he also knew what questions to ask people during interviews. He was active in what remained of Jewish society and was a leader of social programs to help Jews. He was a professional and teacher who could train people for the huge task that lay before them. He also knew that it was important to write down people's accounts immediately. Memory is subjective, especially during trying times such as World War II. Ringelblum didn't want the "before" to be erased by the "after."

It was important to Ringelblum that the archive contain more than just passages composed by scholars and professional writers. He valued historical objectivity and didn't want the interpretations of outside observers to cloud what was really happening to average

In this photograph that was part of the Oneg Shabbat archive assembled by Emmanuel Ringelblum, Jewish police can be seen monitoring a group of Jews in the Warsaw ghetto.

people in the ghetto. He and his team surveyed ghetto residents in order to include a complete and accurate picture of what was happening to European Jews during the war.

A friend of Ringelblum's, Rabbi Simon Huberband, kept his own notes. He wrote these notes in the margins of religious texts to hide them from the Nazis. Ringelblum himself addressed all his notes as letters to friends, family, or colleagues. A letter describing a day's misery was much less liable to get him killed than a stash of notes capturing all the pain and suffering of Warsaw's Jews.

There was a danger to Ringelblum's task. He could not accept just anyone into his organization. If the news leaked out and the Nazis found out what he and his team were doing, they would be killed. Worse, their archive would be destroyed and the world would never know the truth of what was happening to Polish Jews. Ringelblum needed trustworthy people who knew how to keep quiet. No journalists would be allowed. They were famous for being open with people and information. Also, no one from the *Judenrat* (the German-formed Jewish Council that would soon govern the ghetto) would be recruited. Their ability to be threatened with death or bribed for information made them dangerous to a group of secret writers.

Ringelblum began recruiting people for his organization according to certain criteria. He wanted the staff to be made up of people from different parts of Poland. It was also important that they come from various professions and social classes. He wanted economists, doctors, lawyers, and religious leaders. Ringelblum needed this cross section of people in order to collect a cross section of documents and oral accounts of what was happening across Poland. The social historian in Ringelblum had been activated, and he knew the most valuable pieces of information would come from the widest variety of people that could be found.

Ringelblum recruited dozens of people. Many didn't even know what they would be doing. Ringelblum had to determine that they would be good for the job before he told them the secret of the organization. Once he had people in place, Ringelblum taught them how to interview people. They had to learn to determine what information was important and how to organize the information they gathered. Ringelblum didn't want the archive to be merely witnesses' accounts of crimes (though these were important, of course). He wanted to document the economic, health, and social injustices that Jews suffered under the Nazis.

By May 1940, Ringelblum had found his staff for the archive. It was a secret organization that needed a secret name. Since the group met each Saturday, they named themselves Oneg Shabbat (Yiddish for "Sabbath Celebrants"). They knew that this name would not reveal the group's true nature to the Nazis. The Nazis knew that Jews honored their Sabbath day, Saturday. They

Emmanuel Ringelblum

Heard today . . . from someone who visited the Lodz Ghetto. The people there all look like beggars, hunchbacked, starving; many people are now receiving letters telling them of the death of relatives [in work camps] . . . In the street met Mandeltort, a manufacturer I know from Lodz. He was hunchbacked, leaning on a stick like a beggar . . . Rumkowski [head of the Lodz Jewish Council] is said to have ordered everyone in the Lodz Ghetto to give him their furs, under threat of imprisonment. The people of Lodz sold all their furs for a song. For example, they took 50 marks for a fur that could be sold for 1,000 zlotys in Warsaw . . . You see mobs of children in rags begging in the street nowadays . . . Walking down Leszno Street, every few steps you come across people lying at the street corner, frozen, begging.

Taken from the Oneg Shabbat archive

knew Jews prayed on the Sabbath. Oneg Shabbat would mean nothing suspicious to the Nazis. This was the perfect disguise for Oneg Shabbat's real purpose. Ringelblum and his "society of brothers" met each Saturday to review the notes from the week before. The archive quickly grew.

Moving into the Ghetto

On October 13, 1940, a law was passed to gather all Jews into one area of Warsaw. The announcement of the law was especially humiliating because it was made public on Yom Kippur—the highest of Jewish holy days. The Nazis often passed such laws on Jewish holy days.

Jews living throughout Warsaw had just thirty days to report to the walled-in ghetto. Christians living in the ghetto area had to leave. Thousands of businesses were closed because of the ghetto law. Poles and Germans living in Warsaw complained, but the Nazis

Jews being gathered for deportation from the Krakow ghetto

didn't care. They wanted to imprison the Jews and steal their belongings.

Jews could bring into the ghetto only what they could carry. Members of one family who arrived at the ghetto gates with a cart carrying suitcases and furniture were murdered on the spot. As hundreds of thousands of Jews left other parts of the city, Poles and Nazis moved into Jewish homes and used their property.

Ringelblum and his family already lived in the area that became the ghetto. They did not have to leave their apartment. Like other Jews, however, they suffered humiliation when soldiers beat them in the streets or stole their property.

When all the Jews of Warsaw had been moved into the ghetto, the gates were shut and locked. Guards stood inside and outside the gates. The Jews were now separated from the outside world. Almost 400,000 Jews now lived inside the ghetto. It would get more crowded as more Jews were found and deported from the countryside. Only a few thousand Jews were used each day for slave labor; the rest were isolated from Polish society, and most had lost their means to earn a living.

After the first weeks of turmoil, the Jews began to adjust to life in the ghetto. Ringelblum's self-help organization continued to operate. Tens of thousands of

Prisoners of the Warsaw ghetto wait in line to buy hot tea from a vendor.

people were homeless and had nothing. The JDC and other organizations were the only means of help for these people. Others lived on what they had previously saved and could smuggle into the ghetto. There were wealthy people who survived on hidden cash.

Anyone with an ability to sew, make shoes, or do anything that was of value to imprisoned people could make some money that would help them to survive. People began to sell their possessions. They became street vendors, taking their clothing, books, pots, and pans down to the sidewalk and setting them out for people who had spare money or food. Beggars filled the streets, side by side with former society men and women.

Through all of this, the ghetto seemed to have some benefits. Now that the Nazis had the Jews where they wanted them, the mass terror that had become a part of everyday life since the occupation began to calm down. Polish thugs could not beat or kill Jews in the street as they once had. Jewish policemen, not Nazis, patrolled the ghetto streets. The Nazis generally ignored the Jews for the time being. But there were still beatings and murders each day; such terror never stopped and would get much worse after only a few months. Daily life, however, became more livable for the Jews. This was almost three years before the Final Solution began. Forced labor continued, and low rations starved people to death, yet the ghetto began to grow into its own community.

4. Ghetto Life

Ringelblum called the ghetto a "free society of slaves." Now that the Nazis had turned their attention elsewhere, he and the Oneg Shabbat could focus more effort on the archive. Of course, they still had to work in secret, but now they had fewer eyes watching for any crimes being committed. The most feared group of Nazis was the Gestapo (secret police). These men were killers who used the smallest, alleged crime as an excuse to murder Jews. Ringelblum recorded the following event in his journal: "Tonight, Dr. Cooperman was shot for being out after eight o'clock. He had a pass." Such irrational brutality was common, so Jews tried to avoid confrontation with the Gestapo and

Nazi soldiers. Cut off from the world, these Jews began to live as a jailed society.

A Society Grows

Headed by former Jewish leaders who had to answer to the Nazis, the *Judenrat* governed the Warsaw ghetto. The *Judenrat* had a police force, oversaw the hospitals, and collected taxes. The Nazis used the *Judenrat* to rule the ghetto for several reasons: They thought ghetto social order would be better established through self-government; they didn't want to waste precious manpower by using many soldiers to guard the Jews; and the soldiers they had were needed to fight the war. Ghetto residents breathed a sigh of relief that their own people were in charge. This way, they would not have to endure the constant beatings and humiliation that German and Polish police had given them outside the ghetto.

The Nazis allowed the *Judenrat* to govern the ghetto but also forced them to spy on the

In the Warsaw ghetto, the *Judenrat* ran the hospitals and police force and collected taxes.

ghetto residents and to pass on rumors or lies about their future. These lies and rumors helped to confuse the ghetto Jews. Though not as severe as physical beatings, this was another method of terrorizing Jews.

The *Judenrat* also had the job of aiding Polish Jews in need of money, food, clothing, and housing. It might seem strange that the Nazis allowed aid to continue while they were killing and enslaving Jews. It is important to remember that the Nazis were intent on keeping social order within the ghetto; they didn't want riots. Allowing riots and killings would only hurt the Nazis' use of Jews as slave labor. They wanted a calm but terrified and obedient society of Jews that could be used for whatever purpose the Nazis desired.

Later, when the ghetto Jews were deported to the death camps, and reality hit the remaining citizens of the ghetto, order did break down and people hid, rather than go to work at labor camps or factories. For now, however, people began to live as best they could under terrible conditions.

Forming Schools and Social Groups

The Nazis expected the Jews to do nothing in the ghetto except live or die. Political and religious organizations were outlawed inside the ghetto. Even schools were illegal. None of these laws, however, kept the Jews from secretly organizing dozens of schools and social groups. Ringelblum served on committees that formed both social groups and schools to educate children and adults. Now teachers had work to do, even if they could not be paid.

Teaching the ghetto children their regular lessons was the first order of business. The ghetto residents didn't know how long they would live in the walled inner city, but they were not going to neglect their children's education. Under secrecy, children learned history, mathematics, and literature. They were taught Yiddish and were educated in the Torah (Hebrew holy book). Books were not plentiful, but the teachers and students made do with what they had.

Adult study groups, where Yiddish and Hebrew were taught, also formed. Literature and religion were studied. People began to give and attend lectures. Discussion and learning were things that kept people busy and passed the time while they hoped and prayed for the Nazis to lose the war. Of course, the ghetto residents wanted to return to a normal life. Most knew that Jews had been persecuted throughout history, but they held to the belief that all hardships would eventually pass. And they had faith that, if Ringelblum's archive reached an audience, there would never be a hardship like this again.

Jüdische Soziale Selbsthilfe
KIELCE
Żydowska Samopomoc Społeczna

Dział dożyw. dzieci.

Leg. Nr

upoważnia do korzystania
z kuchni Ż. S. S.
ŚNIADANIA

Nazwisko i imię 1600 śniadań
Adres dziennie

Miesiąc maj 1941 r.

31	30	29

A child's identification card entitled the holder to rations—in this case, only breakfast.

Each street in the ghetto formed a house committee. The house committees ran community kitchens and opened homes for homeless children and the aged. Incoming refugees were cared for as best they could be. Those without money often had to live on the street. Others were moved into overcrowded buildings. Every kind of supply was scarce, but each person helped another in some way. Jews had lived among themselves for centuries; they were used to being a part of a self-helping society.

Ringelblum was a director of the Jewish Organization for Social Care (known as "Self-Help"). Self-Help was considered more trustworthy than the *Judenrat*'s Social Welfare Department. People knew the *Judenrat* contained various Nazi spies and collaborators. Also, the Social Welfare Department mainly helped labor camp workers, factory workers, and orphans. Self-Help, on the other hand, worked to help the neediest people. These included refugees, children, and the hungry.

Self-Help received its money from the Red Cross, the Polish Food Commission, and JDC centers throughout Europe.

Ringelblum worked tirelessly for Self-Help. He made the rounds to various orphanages, House Committees, and the many religious groups that had formed inside the ghetto. People always asked for more money, food, and goods. Ringelblum had to explain each time he visited that Self-Help was doing the best it possibly could. He encouraged patience among the many people he visited. There was only so much of everything to go around, and everyone had to share and be prepared to survive on little or nothing.

Counting the Dead

Ringelblum took extra care to document deaths that occurred in the ghetto. Eyewitness accounts of murders were always coming in to Oneg Shabbat. Ringelblum also wanted to

A starving child begs in the street of the Warsaw ghetto.

document death by starvation, disease, the cold (hundreds of people froze to death on the streets and in homes during the winter), and deaths in the labor camps.

Normally, a city of almost half a million people could expect about five hundred deaths each month. In January 1941, almost nine hundred Jews died in the ghetto. Three months later, more than two thousand died. In June, four thousand Jews died. In January 1942, more than five thousand died.

Most of these deaths were caused by starvation or disease brought on by starvation or poor living conditions. Although the Nazis were in charge of feeding the ghetto Jews, they thought that food was too valuable to waste on them. So Jews were fed starvation diets. A non-dieting person should have at least 2,500 calories per day to stay healthy; ghetto residents were given only 184. To live, Jews smuggled food into the ghetto from outside sources.

Underground Groups

Oneg Shabbat was just one important underground (secret and illegal) group working in the Warsaw ghetto. Ringelblum understood the importance of the growing archive, but he knew that there were even more important needs to be met for ghetto residents. Often, the only way to help people was through activities that the Nazis deemed illegal.

Ringelblum's Self-Help organization worked both legally and illegally. Staff working to get money from outside sources used the same offices at night to record notes for Oneg Shabbat. Storefronts used for soup kitchens during the day became schools at night.

Underground political groups sprang up overnight. Each group held its own lectures and meetings. At first, these groups met secretly, at night, in apartments or basements. Each political group also published its own underground newspaper. Most of these newspapers were only a page long, but they contained news that people desperately needed to hear. These newspapers were often delivered in secret. One paper might pass through ten or even twenty hands. Some newspapers were taken from building to building. The delivery person would wait while the residents read the paper, then he would deliver it to the next building.

Ringelblum and Oneg Shabbat saved copies of these underground newspapers. Sometimes the members wondered how "underground" they really were. After a few months, people were openly passing out these makeshift newspapers on the ghetto streets and talking politics on street corners. The Nazis didn't punish them as long as they got their quota of forced laborers each day.

Smuggling

Ghetto residents and organized groups smuggled in food, goods, and coal in order to eat, make extra money, and survive the cold. Without the smuggling system, thousands more people would have starved or frozen to death during the ghetto's three-year existence.

Many smugglers were individuals who brought in small amounts of food to feed themselves or their families. These smugglers left the ghetto each day for labor in city factories. Outside the ghetto, they were able to buy small bits of food or goods from sympathetic Poles. They risked their lives each night when they brought in half a loaf of bread or some cheese.

Other smugglers were large, organized groups that brought in huge quantities of food. These groups were responsible for feeding hundreds of thousands of people.

At first, smuggling goods into the ghetto was fairly easy. The ghetto had twenty-two gates, guarded inside by Jewish and Polish police and outside by German guards. Packages were hidden among regular shipments of "legal" goods and factory deliveries. Often, goods would be brought in after the guards were bribed. Soon, though, the guards were ordered to stop all illegal goods from entering the ghetto.

When the gates closed to the high-traffic smuggling, people went underground—literally. Tunnels were dug from ghetto cellars to the Aryan (non-Jewish) side of Warsaw. Polish merchants and smugglers ran their trade through these tunnels.

The ghetto walls were also a place through which smugglers could operate. Smugglers knocked out enough bricks in the wall for goods to come through at night. The bricks could be replaced each night without notice.

Hundreds of smugglers were caught and immediately executed. Their bodies were left on the street to discourage others. When one smuggling operation was discovered, another would quickly take its place. Smugglers became wealthy in the ghetto. Ringelblum's

Young Jewish men conduct an illegal business deal over a ghetto wall.

Self-Help agency benefited from these smugglers. Self-Help bought food that fed many thousands of starving people.

Shopping, Street Life, and Entertainment

The huge quantities of smuggled goods entering the ghetto allowed businesses to keep operating for a time. People with money shopped at stores that sold canned goods and bread. Coffeehouses continued to serve people. Citizens gathered on the street to look at displays of illegal goods for sale or trade.

At the same time, the young people of the ghetto tried to carry on with their lives. They wanted to meet people, discuss ideas and politics, and maybe even fall in love. One ghetto street became a place for strolling couples. There was a courtyard, where chairs and benches were set out for sunbathing. Young and old alike used these places to gain a sense of normalcy in the midst of their disrupted lives.

Plays and satires (spoofs) were staged in the streets for entertainment. Jewish folklore was often used to parody the plight that people suffered in the ghetto. Ghetto residents developed mottoes, told jokes, and wrote and sang songs about ghetto life. Any kind of entertainment was a diversion to keep their minds off the brutal lives they led.

The Reality of the Ghetto

Most of what we know of ghetto life comes from Ringelblum's notes and the Oneg Shabbat archive. Ringelblum wanted to record a full description of life there. He portrayed the strengths of the Jewish people by documenting every angle of ghetto life: the education programs, social clubs, and religious groups; the news information sources, deaths, and murders; the lack of food to nourish people; and the lack of coal to heat their homes. This was ghetto reality. Jewish strength was always measured against Jewish suffering, and the suffering outweighed the strength by a wide margin.

Friday night, some eight or nine people were killed. One of them was a man called Wilner (from 11 Mylna Street) who lay sick in bed. He could barely crawl out of bed at the command of the hangmen; he sat down on a chair, unable to move any further. So they threw him out of the second-floor window, together with the chair, shooting after him as he fell. In the same apartment three other men were shot (a brother-in-law of [Wilner] called Rudnicki, his son, and another person). Reason unknown.

Taken from the Oneg Shabbat archive

The Nazis wanted to starve and work the Jews to death, and they were successful. There were few acts of defiance against what the Nazis did to the Jews because any sign of resistance brought about reprisals that killed dozens of people who were just trying to survive. The daily work gangs took thousands of people out of the ghetto and into factories or labor camps. At day's end, hundreds did not return; many died while working. They were starving and in very poor health. Their bodies gave out, and they died. Others were shot for some misdeed or on a whim. The Jews had no chance against the Nazis.

Deportation to Treblinka

By the summer of 1942, ghetto residents had long known that only a miracle would save them. The war dragged on (it would not end for three more years), and Nazi brutality was increasing. The Nazis had murdered hundreds of thousands of European Jews. Most Jews knew that it was only a matter of time before their turn came. They believed that they would die from starvation, the cold, or a Nazi bullet. They did not know the Nazis had devised a new, systematic plan to kill them.

In July 1942, mass deportations of the ghetto Jews began. The Final Solution—Hitler's plan to exterminate all Jews—had gone into effect, and the Warsaw ghetto's remaining 350,000 residents were the largest group of Jews being held in one place. The Nazis had decided that no Jew would be allowed to live in Europe. Between July 1942 and April 1943, more than 330,000 Warsaw Jews were deported to the Treblinka death camp. The Nazis built Treblinka for the sole purpose of gassing Jews and burning their bodies in ovens called crematoriums to destroy the evidence.

At first, many Jews did not realize that they were being taken to their deaths. They were told that a new work camp was open and that they would be fed for their labor. Thousands believed this; each day they were crowded onto railway cars and shuttled to their deaths.

Ringelblum and Oneg Shabbat learned the truth from Jews who had escaped from

Treblinka. Immediately, people began to hide from the Nazis as they moved into the streets each day to round up Jews to send off to Treblinka.

Ringelblum was not one of the Jews sent to die. Because he was a man of importance in the community, he was allowed to remain in the ghetto. Other important people stayed alive because of their status. They often bribed the soldiers who came to take them away. Later, as more and more Jews were sent away, Ringelblum and other members of Oneg Shabbat hid in secret bunkers within the ghetto. By April 1943, no one was safe. Ringelblum had to somehow escape the ghetto with his wife and son.

5. The Nazis Close In

At the beginning of 1943, Oneg Shabbat decided that it needed to do something with its archive. The archive had grown to thousands of pages. It included dozens of newspapers, journals, leaflets, decrees, and photographs. The plan was to write a summary of the archive to organize what had been collected for the past three years. This was a huge and dangerous project. The Oneg Shabbat staff lived in constant fear of being caught. If the Nazis discovered the archive, the memory and eyewitness statements of Polish Jews would be lost forever.

The Oneg Shabbat editorial committee decided to organize the archive into four sections. Each would be a summary of a different part of ghetto life.

At hour-long editorial sessions we mulled over the main points in each of the themes. What we wished to do was to draw the author's attention to specific trends, and to indicate the lines along which he could develop his theme . . . Some of the themes we worked out dealt with the Law and Order Service [Jewish police], corruption and demoralization in the Ghetto, community activity . . . the educational system [and] special problems affecting young people and women.

Taken from the Oneg Shabbat archive

Ringelblum began to summarize two parts himself: the cultural and literary history of the Warsaw ghetto and Polish Jews.

A Chance to Fight Back

Since the first days of the ghetto's existence, some underground leaders had wanted to train young men to fight against the Nazis.

They had planned to form fighting groups to surprise the Nazis. If they could not defeat the Nazis, at least they could kill some. Other leaders warned against this. They said that any uprising would bring Nazi revenge. Innocent people would be murdered in return for the lives of just a few Nazis.

By the end of 1942, only 40,000 Jews remained in the ghetto. The underground groups decided that fighting was the only way to survive. They had watched and done little while more than 90 percent of the ghetto Jews were sent to the Treblinka gas chambers. The war raged on. No one was going to help them. It was time to fight.

Thousands of Jews were still alive because they were hiding in secret cellars. Others had been living in sewers and in attics of abandoned buildings for months. When a plan to fight back took shape, many came out of hiding to join the resistance.

Ringelblum helped lead the resistance against the Nazis. He strongly disagreed with the older generation of Jews who felt that their goal should be to hide, to obey, or to do whatever it took to survive the Nazi regime. Ringelblum and many young people felt that resistance would grant them respect. They believed an honorable death would be better than giving in to Nazi demands and being passively led to slaughter, or—worse—standing

Polish resistance fighters escort a captured SS trooper during the Warsaw ghetto uprising.

as symbols of the inferiority of Jews before the rest of the world and future generations.

Ringelblum was the head of the leftist Po'alei Zion, a small political group. There were more than a dozen such political groups inside the ghetto. Each group recruited young men and women to fight. On July 23, 1942, all of these groups met to decide how they could fight back against the Nazi deportations. The Jewish Fighting Organization (ZOB) was formed. Recruits were trained to fight in the streets by Jews who had once been soldiers themselves (some had fought on the side of Germany in World War I). The ZOB bought guns and hand grenades with help from Polish resistance units outside the ghetto. The Polish resistance also helped with money and escape routes for the ZOB.

The Ringelblum archive saved a poster that was handed out to residents by the ZOB in early January 1943:

We are going out to war! We are among those who have set themselves the goal of rousing the people . . .

He who fights for his life has a chance of being saved: He who rules out resistance from the start is already lost, doomed to a degrading death in the suffocation machine at Treblinka.

Rouse yourselves to war: Find the courage to indulge in acts of madness: Put a stop to the degrading resignation expressed by such statements as: "We are all bound to die." That is a lie: For we have been sentenced to live! We, too, are deserving of life. You merely must know how to fight for it!

Taken from the Oneg Shabbat archive

The first uprising took place on January 18, 1943. That morning, Jews heading out for a day of forced labor discovered that the gates had been blocked by German troops. They knew that another mass deportation was about to happen. They quickly went back through the ghetto warning people.

Thousands of Jews went into hiding. The ZOB was caught off guard: They had not thought a deportation would happen on the day of their attack. Only a few ZOB groups gathered to fight. The fighting took place on the streets near the railway yard used to deport Jews. The Jewish fighters walked with others in the streets toward the *Umschlagplatz* (trading place)—the place where Jews were crowded onto boxcars for the train ride to Treblinka. Along the way, the fighters left the lines and hid in alleyways or doorways. Each took aim at one soldier or guard. A signal was given and shots rang out.

The battle lasted only ten or fifteen minutes. Reports from that day vary, but it is believed that twelve guards and Nazi soldiers were killed. Ten more were wounded. The Jewish fighters lost nine men.

The fighting slowed this newest deportation. The Nazis had wanted to round up eight thousand Jews; they deported fewer than three thousand. The ZOB saw this action as a victory. Others in the ghetto were worried that the Nazis would seek revenge and try to kill them all.

This small success filled the ZOB with hope. They knew they couldn't defeat the Nazis, but they could hurt them. The Nazis were outraged. They began to plan for the total destruction of the ghetto and all the Jews still living inside.

The Last Days of the Ghetto

During the January uprising, Ringelblum continued to work on his summary sections of the archive. Other Oneg Shabbat members could not continue. Some had been killed in the streets. Others had been rounded up during the deportations and sent to the death camp.

> *The O.S. [Oneg Shabbat] work was interrupted. Only a handful of our friends kept pencil in hand and continued to write about what was happening in Warsaw in those calamitous [disastrous] days. But the work was too holy for us, it was too deep in our hearts, the O.S. was too important for the community—we could not stop.*
>
> Taken from the Oneg Shabbat archive

The remaining Oneg Shabbat archivists began to collect eyewitness accounts of Jews sent to Treblinka. Ringelblum called Treblinka "the charnel house of European Jewry," meaning it was a repository for bodies of the dead.

The ZOB prepared for more battles with the Nazis. They expected more deportations and would no longer go without a fight. People began to build bunkers in which to hide and fight, should the Nazis find them. A battle was brewing that would surprise the Nazis and mark the beginning of the end of the Warsaw ghetto.

Meanwhile, Oneg Shabbat decided that the archive should be sealed and buried. The summaries were not yet completed, but time was running out. The editors collected tin boxes and rubberized milk cans. The archive, along with Ringelblum's notes, were placed inside. Once sealed, the containers were buried in three separate places inside the ghetto.

Ringelblum's Escape

As the resistance worked to prepare for another battle, its leaders wanted to smuggle Ringelblum and his family to safety outside the ghetto. There is no record of his thoughts about leaving the ghetto. Some historians believe that he argued with the ZOB leaders. His writings and his character suggest that he would have wanted to stay on in the ghetto to the very end. The ZOB leaders, however, knew that Ringelblum's life and knowledge of the ghetto were much too important to risk. If he could survive the Nazi Jew-hunters and the war, he could personally tell the world what had happened all around him.

In April 1943, Ringelblum and his family escaped the ghetto with help from the Polish resistance. They were hiding in the Aryan side of Warsaw when the final armed revolt of the Jewish fighters began on April 19.

The Last Revolt and Destruction of the Ghetto

On April 18, the ZOB heard that Nazi troops were going to march through the ghetto. Jewish combat groups took position in buildings overlooking several streets. On April 19, the first Nazi soldiers marched down

Nalewki Street, singing songs. The combat troops opened fire with guns and grenades. This first clash killed and wounded many Nazis. They scattered back down the street and tried to regroup. The Jewish resisters fought against the advancing Nazis and were able to kill many more soldiers.

This first battle was the beginning of many battles over the next four weeks. The all-out revolt of the ZOB lasted until May 16. Near the end, the German command sent in regular troops and tanks to destroy the ghetto. They marched block by block, bombing and setting fire to every building. Most of the remaining few thousand ghetto Jews died during these battles.

The ghetto was leveled by the bombings. Later, the Nazis built a concentration camp where the ghetto once stood. They continued to find Jews hiding in underground bunkers and the sewers. Each Jew they found was immediately shot or sent to a death camp.

6. A Noble Death

Emmanuel Ringelblum tried to help the ZOB from his hideout in the Aryan section of Warsaw. In May 1943, the Polish government-in-exile was living in London, England. The government leaders received a message from the Jewish fighters asking for help. Ringelblum's name was one of the three signatures on the message.

Ringelblum returned to the ghetto on a short mission during the final weeks of the Jewish revolt. He was captured by the Nazis and sent to the slave labor camp at Trawniki with several other ghetto fighters. His wife and son were still hiding in the Aryan side of Warsaw.

A Second Escape

Ringelblum worked in the Trawniki camp for only a few weeks. Jews in the camp knew who

Ringelblum was, and a plan was made to smuggle him to safety. The Jewish underground helped Ringelblum escape. Once safely away from the camp, Ringelblum returned to Warsaw.

Ringelblum was able to get false papers that identified him as an Aryan. These papers allowed him to continue some of his work in Warsaw. He, along with his wife and son and thirty other Jews, lived in a bunker beneath a Polish gardener's house on Grojecka Street.

Ringelblum continued to write in his underground home. He began to record a history of the Trawniki labor camp and those Jews who had worked and died there. He also began to write a history of the Jewish Combat Organization in Poland. The resistance movement that the Polish Jews had formed amazed Ringelblum. He had much respect for those who had given their lives to fight against a system that had already killed millions.

Luck Runs Out

Ringelblum lived in the underground bunker from July 1943 until March 7, 1944. He had one more chance to escape Warsaw. In the fall of 1943, the Polish underground in Warsaw sent a list of nineteen names to the Polish government-in-exile. Those listed were the remaining leaders of the Jewish underground. The Polish government agreed to rescue these people in January 1944. Unfortunately, only three of the people on that list were still alive. Ringelblum was one of them.

The three remaining underground leaders refused to be rescued. They had come this far and would stay until the very end. Ringelblum wrote, "We must fulfill our duty to society."

On March 7, the German police discovered the Jews hiding beneath the Polish gardener's house. The gardener's mistress had betrayed them after an argument with her lover. The Jews were taken to the Pawiak prison in Warsaw.

Defiant to the End

Emmanuel Ringelblum was murdered along with his wife and son a few days after their capture. What happened between the time of his capture and his death is not exactly known. There are two stories of his final days. Both stories show that Ringelblum stayed true

A German firing squad executes two Polish prisoners against a wall in the Warsaw ghetto.

to his own character to the end. Even in the face of death, he would not bow to the Nazis. The archive would have to stand on its own as a testament to European and Polish Jewry.

The first story comes from an eyewitness account. Julian Hirszhaut was an inmate at Pawiak prison when the Jews who had been discovered were brought in. He and other prisoners worked as tailors and shoemakers for the Germans. Some prisoners recognized Ringelblum from the ghetto. Many others knew of him. He was known from his work with the Self-Help welfare society.

Some of the prisoners decided that they would try to bribe the guard to get Ringelblum released for special work duty. They told the guard that Ringelblum was a shoemaker and would be important to the Nazi war effort. One of these men was Hirszhaut. He was able to get into the cell where Ringelblum and his son were kept. Hirszhaut recounted:

> On his lap Ringelblum was holding a handsome boy. This was his son Uri.

> When I approached Ringelblum, I told him, without losing any time, whose messenger I was. I remember how astonished Ringelblum was to learn that there were still Jews in Pawiak. Then I told him that we were making attempts to take him in with us. "And what will happen to him?" he asked, pointing his finger at his son. "And what will happen to my wife who is in the women's section?" What could I answer him? My silence conveyed the truth to him.

Ringelblum refused the prisoners' help. He told Hirszhaut how the Gestapo had tortured him. They had wanted to know the names of his contacts on the Aryan side of Warsaw. Ringelblum told Hirszhaut that he would rather die like all the Jews he had known. Hirszhaut then told how Ringelblum finally said to him in a "voice that was broken from despair, 'What is this little boy guilty of?'—

and he again pointed his finger at his son—'It breaks my heart to think of him.'"

The prisoners ignored Ringelblum's wish to stay with his family and the other captured Jews. They, too, knew of his importance to the memory of Polish Jewry. They bribed the guard anyway.

The next day, the captured Jews were taken inside the ruined ghetto and executed. Ringelblum and his wife and child were murdered with them. The guard that had taken the bribe told the Pawiak prisoners: "I understand he wasn't a shoemaker after all."

The other account of Ringelblum's death tells how the Gestapo knew who he was all along. They tortured him and his wife and son to try and find out where the archive had been buried. None of them would talk.

Emmanuel Ringelblum was a man who, above all, found the strength to remain objective and hopeful in emotional and horrifying times. He found his life's purpose during history's darkest hour, a time that, ironically, led to his death. His chief mission—to record accurately the Jewish experience of World War II—should be considered a fight as important as battling hunger or the enemy.

Although Ringelblum participated in the resistance to uphold the dignity of the Jewish people, his greatest battle was the fight to preserve history. He was convinced that the story of Jewish suffering, no matter how terrible, was universal, and that the story of that suffering could be put to use educating future generations. Oneg Shabbat proved that nothing that was Jewish was futile—that even in the face of no future, history is vital.

Timeline

1900	Emmanuel Ringelblum is born.
1914–1918	World War I is fought.
1925	Hitler publishes *Mein Kampf* ("My Struggle"), a work that blames Jews for all the harm that came to Germany after World War I.
1932	Nazi Party wins many seats in the Reichstag, allowing them a role in ruling Germany.
1933	Adolf Hitler is named chancellor of Germany; Emmanuel Ringelblum begins collecting accounts that document the history of Nazi crimes against Jews.
1936	New laws are enacted in Germany to take away Jewish rights of citizenship, work, and land ownership in

	Germany. Ringelblum begins work with Jewish Self-Help organization in Poland.
1939	Nazis invade Poland and defeat the Polish army within six weeks; World War II begins.
1940	New Polish law orders Warsaw Jews to move into ghetto formed on the north side of the city; Oneg Shabbat formed inside the ghetto.
1942	The Nazis' Final Solution begins; thousands of Warsaw Jews are sent to Treblinka death camp to be killed. Jewish Fighting Organization (ZOB) formed in Warsaw ghetto.
1943	Oneg Shabbat begins organizing all archive material into four sections; Ringelblum edits two sections himself. First Jewish armed attack against Nazis inside Warsaw ghetto. German army enters Warsaw ghetto with troops and tanks; the ghetto is bombed until it is leveled.
1944	March 7: German police discover Ringelblum family and thirty other Jews living beneath a Polish gardener's house. Nazis execute

	Ringelblum, his wife, and his son a few days after their capture.
1945	Soviet army overruns Warsaw; Nazis defeated in March. Treblinka is liberated.
1946	First documents from Oneg Shabbat archive found in rubble of Warsaw.
1958	Emmanuel Ringelblum's *Notes from the Warsaw Ghetto* is published.

Glossary

archive
A collection of records or documents that gives details about a period of time or event in history.

Aryan
Non-Jewish people with Nordic features that the Nazis considered to be the "master race."

death camp
A prison where people are taken to be killed. The Nazis used death camps to kill Jews and other "criminals" whom they deemed unfit to live. Prisoners were gassed and then burned in ovens.

Final Solution
A term used by the Nazis to describe the systematic and total destruction of European Jews.

Gestapo (*Geheime Staatspolizei*)
The Nazi secret police in charge of keeping order in the streets of all German and occupied territories.

ghetto
Under the Nazis, an area of a city where Jews were kept apart from the rest of the population.

Judenrat
The Jewish government body that oversaw the Warsaw ghetto from 1940 to 1943. Similar *Judenrat* groups oversaw other ghettos.

Oneg Shabbat
Yiddish for "Sabbath Celebrants." A group of writers and editors in the Warsaw ghetto (1940–1943) who gathered documents and interviewed eyewitnesses to record Nazi crimes against Polish Jews.

SS (*Schutzstaffel*)
German for "protection squad," the SS was in charge of capturing Jews and putting them in ghettos or concentration camps. Later in the war, the SS was in charge of the Final Solution.

Zionist
Someone who believes that a national Jewish state should be created.

ZOB (Jewish Fighting Organization)
The organization that led the many smaller groups of Jewish resistance fighters against the Nazis in the Warsaw ghetto.

For More Information

Simon Wiesenthal Center and Museum of Tolerance
1399 South Roxbury Drive
Los Angeles, CA 90035
(800) 900-9036
Web site: http://www.wiesenthal.com

Survivors of the Shoah Visual History Foundation
P.O. Box 3168
Los Angeles, CA 90078-3168
(818) 777-4673
Web site: http://www.vhf.org

United States Holocaust Memorial Museum
100 Raoul Wallenberg Place SW
Washington, DC 20024-2126
(202) 488-0400
Web site: http://www.ushmm.org

Web Sites

The Holocaust History Project Homepage
http://www.holocaust-history.org

Holocaust Memorial Center: Illuminating the Past
http://www.holocaustcenter.org

Voice Vision: Holocaust Survivor Oral Histories
http://holocaust.umd.umich.edu

Yad Vashem
http://www.yadvashem.org

For Further Reading

Adler, David A. *Child of the Warsaw Ghetto.* New York: Holiday House, 1995.

Block, Gay, and Malka Drucker. *Rescuers: Portraits of Moral Courage in the Holocaust.* New York: Holmes & Meier, 1992.

Fox, Anne L. *Ten Thousand Children: True Stories Told by Children Who Escaped the Holocaust on the Kindertransport.* West Orange, NJ: Behrman House, 1999.

Frank, Anne. *The Diary of a Young Girl.* B. M. Mooyaart, trans. New York: Bantam,1993.

Geier, Arnold. *Heroes of the Holocaust.* New York: Berkley, 1998.

Georg, Willy. *In the Warsaw Ghetto: Summer 1941.* New York: Aperture Books, 1993.

Gilbert, Martin. *The Holocaust: A History of the Jews of Europe During the Second World War.* New York: Henry Holt, 1985.

Gutman, Israel. *The Jews of Warsaw: 1939–1943.* Bloomington, IN: Indiana University Press, 1982.

For Further Reading

Leapman, Michael. *Witnesses to War: Eight True-Life Stories of Nazi Persecution.* New York: Viking, 1998.

Ringelblum, Emmanuel. *Notes from the Warsaw Ghetto.* Jacob Sloan, ed. New York: Schocken, 1958.

Stadtler, Bea. *The Holocaust: A History of Courage and Resistance.* West Orange, NJ: Behrman House, 1994.

Index

Index

About the Author

Mark Beyer has written more than fifty young adult and children's books. He is currently working on a novel. He lives with his wife in New York City.

Photo Credits

Cover photo and pp. 23, 41 © Yivo Institute for Jewish Research, courtesy of United States Holocaust Memorial Museum Photo Archive (USHMM); p. 4 adapted from map by William L. Nelson, *The Holocaust Encyclopedia,* Yale University Press; p. 7 © Leah Hammerstein Silverstein, courtesy of USHMM; pp. 9, 56, 63 © Yad Vashem Photo Archives, courtesy of USHMM; p. 14 © Hulton Getty Picture Collection; p. 17 © National Archives, courtesy of USHMM; p. 20 © David Wherry, courtesy of USHMM; p. 30 © Amalie Petranker Salsitz, courtesy of USHMM Photo Archives; p. 36 © Yaffa Eliach Collection, Center for Holocaust Studies, donated to the Museum of Jewish Heritage—A Living Memorial to the Holocaust, New York; p. 44 © Archiwum Dokumentocji Mechannizney, courtesy of USHMM; p. 50 © Zydowski Instytut Historyczny Instytut Naukowo-Badawczy, courtesy of USHMM; p. 58 © Bundesarchiv; p. 66 © Rafel Imbro, courtesy of USHMM; p. 69 © Raphael Scharf, courtesy of USHMM; p. 74 © Jerzy Tomaszewski, courtesy of USHMM; p. 84 © courtesy of USHMM Photo Archives; p. 96 © Main Commission for the Prosecution of the Crimes against the Polish Nation, courtesy of USHMM.

Series Design

Cynthia Williamson

Layout

Les Kanturek